THE LIVING MARRIAGE

BY *H. Norman Wright*

THE CHRISTIAN USE OF EMOTIONAL POWER
THE LIVING MARRIAGE

H. NORMAN WRIGHT
COMPILER

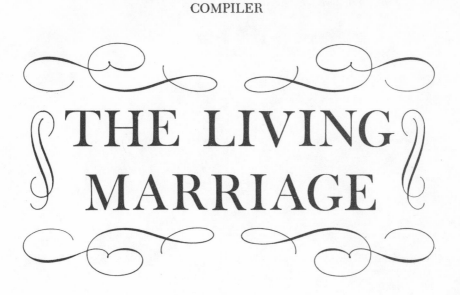

THE LIVING
MARRIAGE

Lessons in Love
From the Living Bible

FLEMING H. REVELL COMPANY

OLD TAPPAN, NEW JERSEY

Library of Congress Cataloging in Publication Data

Wright, H   Norman, comp.
   The living marriage.

   Includes bibliographical references.
    1. Marriage. 2. Marriage—Biblical teaching.
I.   Taylor, Kenneth Nathaniel. The living bible, paraphrased. ̄Selections. II. Title.
BV835.W74   248'.4   74-31460
ISBN 0-8007-0722-2

TO my wife, Joycelin,

whom God has used to help fulfill my life
through her encouragement, patience,
love, and acceptance

CONTENTS

ACKNOWLEDGMENTS

All Scripture quotations in this volume are from The Living Bible, Copyright © 1971 by Tyndale House Publishers, Wheaton, Illinois 60187. All rights reserved. Used by permission.

The excerpts from *Cherishable: Love and Marriage* by David W. Augsburger. Copyright © 1971 by Herald Press, Scottdale, Pa. Used by permission.

The excerpt from "Behind Many Flaws of Society, Families That Fail to Function," is reprinted with permission from The National Observer, copyright Dow Jones & Company, Inc., 1964.

The excerpt from *I John, Take Thee Mary* by Robert N. Rodenmayer, © 1962 by The Seabury Press, Inc. Used by permission.

The excerpts from *After You've Said I Do* by Dwight Hervey Small, copyright © 1968 by Fleming H. Revell Company. Used by permission.

The excerpt from THE CREATIVE YEARS by Reuel L. Howe, Copyright © 1959 by The Seabury Press, Inc. Used by permission of the Publisher.

The excerpt from Paul Tournier, *Secrets*, p. 47, © M. E. Bratcher 1965. Used by permission of John Knox Press.

The excerpt from THE MATURE MIND by H. A. Overstreet. Copyright 1949, © 1959 by W. W. Norton & Company, Inc., New York, N.Y. With the permission of the publisher.

The excerpt from *Peace of Mind* by Joshua Loth Liebman, Copyright 1946 by Joshua Loth Liebman. Reprinted by permission of Simon & Schuster.

The excerpt from LETTERS TO KAREN by Charlie Shedd, Copyright © 1965 by Abingdon Press, used by permission.

The excerpts from *Caring Enough to Confront* (a Regal Book) by David Augsburger are reprinted by permission of G/L Publications, Glendale, California 91209. Copyright © 1974 under the title, *The Love Fight*, by Herald Press, Scottdale, Pa. 15683.

The excerpts from *The Art of Loving* by Erich Fromm, copyright © 1956 by Erich Fromm, are used by permission of Harper & Row, Publishers, Inc.

The excerpts from *To Understand Each Other* by Paul Tournier, © 1967 by M. E. Bratcher. Used by permission of John Knox Press.

The excerpts from *Be All You Can Be* by David Augsburger, copyright © 1970 by Creation House, Inc., are used by permission of Creation House, Inc., 429 E. St. Charles Road, P.O. Box 316, Carol Stream, Ill. 60187.

The excerpt from *The Intimate Marriage* by Howard Clinebell, copy-

INTRODUCTION

What does marriage mean to you? What is the purpose of marriage? What can you receive from your marriage relationship? What will you contribute to your marriage relationship? The pattern for a growing and productive marriage is found within God's Word. Not only must one know which Scriptures to build a marriage relationship upon, but effort, determination, and consistency must be employed to translate God's Word into one's behavior and attitudes.

This book has within it selected Scriptures and quotations to help guide you in your marriage. As you read each quotation, think upon the meaning for your life, your marriage. What does this statement say to you and how can you use what is being expressed? As you read the selected Scriptures, attempt to visualize what your individual and married life would be like if these verses were being acted upon. The richest and most productive marriages will be those which reflect the content of these Scriptures in attitude and action. This then is a pattern for your life. Build your marriage upon *the* solid foundation.

MARRIAGE

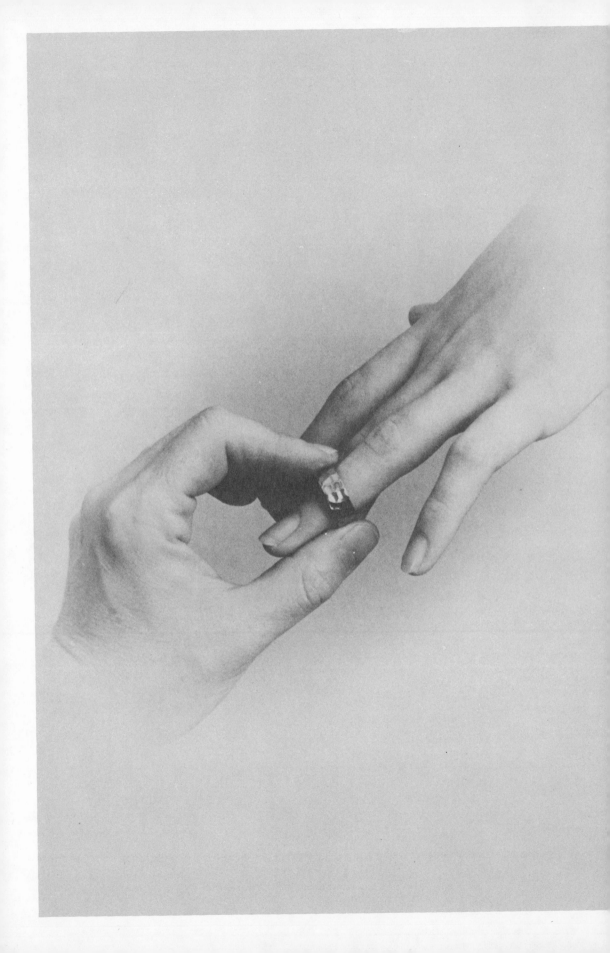

"It isn't a case of marriage having been tried and found wanting. In the 20th century world, true marriage is deeply wanted but largely untried." [1]

"Marriage is a covenant of responsible love, a fellowship of repentance and forgiveness." [2]

"Marriage is a *total* commitment of the *total* person for the *total* life." [3]

"Marriage resembles a pair of shears, so joined that they cannot be separated; often moving in opposite directions, yet always punishing anyone who comes between them." [4]

"Is marriage a private action of two persons in love, or a public act of two pledging a contract? Neither, it is something other. Very much other! Basically, the Christian view of marriage is not that it is primarily or essentially a binding legal and social contract. The Christian understands marriage as a covenant made under God and in the presence of fellow members of the Christian Family. Such a pledge endures, not because of the force of law or the fear of its sanctions, but because an unconditional covenant has been made. A covenant more solemn, more binding, more permanent than any legal contract." [5]

"A system by means of which persons who are sinful and contentious are so caught up by a dream and a purpose bigger than themselves that they work through the years, in spite of repeated disappointment, to make the dream come true." [6]

"Marriage does not demand perfection. But it must be given priority. It is an institution for sinners. No one else need apply. But it finds its finest glory when sinners see it as God's way of leading us through His ultimate curriculum of love and righteousness." [7]

"Marriage introduces a world full of pictures. The selection of a mate is marked by many dreams and wishes. We have our ideas, our conceptions about marriage, about our mate—ideas which we've inherited or collected and which fill us with anticipation. The success or failure of a marriage often depends upon the ability to survive disappointments or to refashion our dreams to fit reality." [8]

"Marriage is not so much a cement as it is a solvent, a freeing-up of this man and this woman to be themselves and to help each other in the process of self-discovery." [9]

MARRIAGE

And the Lord God said, "It isn't good for man to be alone; I will make a companion for him, a helper suited to his needs."

Genesis 2:18-25

So the Lord God formed from the soil every kind of animal and bird, and brought them to the man to see what he would call them; and whatever he called them, that was their name. But still there was no proper helper for the man. Then the Lord God caused the man to fall into a deep sleep, and took one of his ribs and closed up the place from which he had removed it, and made the rib into a woman, and brought her to the man.

"This is it!" Adam exclaimed. "She is part of my own bone and flesh! Her name is 'woman' because she was taken out of a man." This explains why a man leaves his father and mother and is joined to his wife in such a way that the two become one person. Now although the man and his wife were both naked, neither of them was embarrassed or ashamed.

THE VALUE OF A GOOD WIFE

Proverbs

31:10	If you can find a truly good wife, she is worth more than precious gems!
31:11	Her husband can trust her, and she will richly satisfy his needs.
31:12	She will not hinder him, but help him all her life.
31:13	She finds wool and flax and busily spins it.
31:14	She buys imported foods, brought by ship from distant ports.
31:15	She gets up before dawn to prepare breakfast for her household, and plans the day's work for her servant girls.
31:16	She goes out to inspect a field, and buys it; with her own hands she plants a vineyard.
31:17	She is energetic, a hard worker,
31:18	and watches for bargains. She works far into the night!
31:19, 20	She sews for the poor, and generously gives to the needy.
31:21	She has no fear of winter for her household, for she has made warm clothes for all of them.
31:22	She also upholsters with finest tapestry; her own clothing is beautifully made—a purple gown of pure linen.
31:23	Her husband is well known, for he sits in the council chamber with the other civic leaders.
31:24	She makes belted linen garments to sell to the merchants.
31:25	She is a woman of strength and dignity, and has no fear of old age.
31:26	When she speaks, her words are wise, and kindness is the rule for everything she says.
31:27	She watches carefully all that goes on throughout her household, and is never lazy.
31:28	Her children stand and bless her; so does her husband. He praises her with these words: "There are many fine women in the world, but you are the best of them all!"

A worthy wife is her husband's joy and crown; the other kind corrodes his strength and tears down everything he does.

Proverbs 12:4

A wise woman builds her house, while a foolish woman tears hers down by her own efforts.

14:1

The man who finds a wife finds a good thing; she is a blessing to him from the Lord.

18:22

Charm can be deceptive and beauty doesn't last, but a woman who fears and reverences God shall be greatly praised.

31:30

Praise her for the many fine things she does. These good deeds of hers shall bring her honor and recognition from even the leaders of the nations.

31:31

A WIFE'S RELATIONSHIP TO HER HUSBAND

Ephesians

5:21   Honor Christ by submitting to each other.

5:22   You wives must submit to your husbands' leadership in the same way you submit to the Lord.

5:23   For a husband is in charge of his wife in the same way Christ is in charge of his body the church. (He gave his very life to take care of it and be its Savior!)

5:24   So you wives must willingly obey your husbands in everything, just as the church obeys Christ.

Colossians 3:18   You wives, submit yourselves to your husbands, for that is what the Lord has planned for you.

1 Peter 3:1-6   Wives, fit in with your husbands' plans; for then if they refuse to listen when you talk to them about the Lord, they will be won by your respectful, pure behavior. Your godly lives will speak to them better than any words. Don't be concerned about the outward beauty that depends on jewelry, or beautiful clothes, or hair arrangement. Be beautiful inside, in your hearts, with the lasting charm of a gentle and quiet spirit which is so precious to God. That kind of deep beauty was seen in the saintly women of old, who trusted God and fitted in with their husbands' plans. Sarah, for instance, obeyed her husband Abraham, honoring him as head of the house. And if you do the same, you will be following in her steps like good daughters and doing what is right; then you will not need to fear [offending your husbands].

A HUSBAND'S RELATIONSHIP TO HIS WIFE

And you husbands, show the same kind of love to your wives as Christ showed to the church when he died for her,

Ephesians 5:25

to make her holy and clean, washed by baptism and God's Word;

5:26

so that he could give her to himself as a glorious church without a single spot or wrinkle or any other blemish, being holy and without a single fault.

5:27

That is how husbands should treat their wives, loving them as parts of themselves. For since a man and his wife are now one, a man is really doing himself a favor and loving himself when he loves his wife!

5:28

No one hates his own body but lovingly cares for it, just as Christ cares for his body the church, of which we are parts.

5:29, 30

(That the husband and wife are one body is proved by the Scripture which says, "A man must leave his father and mother when he marries, so that he can be perfectly joined to his wife, and the two shall be one.")

5:31

I know this is hard to understand, but it is an illustration of the way we are parts of the body of Christ.

5:32

So again I say, a man must love his wife as a part of himself; and the wife must see to it that she deeply respects her husband—obeying, praising and honoring him.

5:33

And you husbands must be loving and kind to your wives and not bitter against them, nor harsh.

Colossians 3:19

You husbands must be careful of your wives, being thoughtful of their needs and honoring them as the weaker sex. Remember that you and your wife are partners in receiving God's blessings, and if you don't treat her as you should, your prayers will not get ready answers.

1 Peter 3:7

PURE THOUGHTS AND PLANNING ENHANCE A MARRIAGE

Proverbs

12:5   A good man's mind is filled with honest thoughts; an evil man's mind is crammed with lies.

12:8   Everyone admires a man with good sense, but a man with a warped mind is despised.

13:16   A wise man thinks ahead; a fool doesn't, and even brags about it!

16:1, 3, 9   We can make our plans, but the final outcome is in God's hands.
                Commit your work to the Lord, then it will succeed. We should make plans—counting on God to direct us.

27:12   A sensible man watches for problems ahead and prepares to meet them. The simpleton never looks, and suffers the consequences.

YOUR SENSE OF VALUES AND YOUR WORK

The evil man gets rich for the moment, but the good man's reward lasts forever.	Proverbs 11:18
It is possible to give away and become richer! It is also possible to hold on too tightly and lose everything. Yes, the liberal man shall be rich! By watering others, he waters himself.	11:24, 25
Trust in your money and down you go! Trust in God and flourish as a tree!	11:28
Work harder and become a leader; be lazy and never succeed.	12:24
Work brings profit; talk brings poverty!	14:23
A lazy fellow has trouble all through life; the good man's path is easy!	15:19
A little, gained honestly, is better than great wealth gotten by dishonest means.	16:8
The rich man thinks of his wealth as an impregnable defense, a high wall of safety. What a dreamer!	18:11
Better be poor and honest than rich and dishonest.	19:1
A lazy man sleeps soundly—and goes hungry!	19:15
Dishonest gain will never last, so why take the risk?	21:6
Hard work brings prosperity; playing around brings poverty.	28:19
Trying to get rich quick is evil and leads to poverty.	28.22
Don't store up treasures here on earth where they can erode away or may be stolen. Store them in heaven where they will never lose their value, and are safe from thieves. If your profits are in heaven your heart will be there too.	Matthew 6:19-21

LOVE

"There comes a time in the development of every person when he *must* love his neighbor or become a twisted or stunted personality." [1]

"The tragedy of love is not death or separating, but the tragedy of love is indifference." [2]

"Is Love *not*, in Biblical terms, an emotion? It is an orientation, an attitude, of the total personality, 'heart and soul and mind and strength.' It is an outgoing concern for what is loved that seeks to serve and to give." [3]

"To love somebody is not just a strong feeling—it is a decision, it is a judgment, it is a promise." [4]

"Love is an activity; if I love, I am in a constant state of active concern with the loved person." [5]

"The love of a person implies not the possession of that person but the affirmation of that person." [6]

"It is in the very *process* of doing things for others that you begin to fall in love. It is also through the very *process* of doing things with and for others that you stay in love." [7]

"Love is an unconditional commitment to an imperfect person." [8]

EMPATHY

"I know I cannot enter all you feel, nor bear with you the burden of your pain. I can but offer what my love does give: the strength of caring. . . . This I do in quiet ways that on your lonely path you may not walk alone." [9]

"To empathize is to see with the eyes of another, to feel with the heart of another." [10]

"If you have empathy for another you abandon your own self, and seem to become fused with and absorbed in the inner experience of the other person." [11]

"Empathy serves us in two ways. First, it helps us to understand the other person from within. We communicate on a deeper level and apprehend the other person more completely. With this kind of communication we often find ourselves accepting that person and entering into a relationship of appreciation and sympathy. In another sense, empathy becomes for us a source of personal reassurance. We are reassured when we feel that someone has succeeded in feeling himself into our own state of mind. We enjoy the satisfaction of being understood and accepted as persons." [12]

"We want and really need someone who will be involved in our life. When we open that hidden part of ourselves even for a moment, we need someone who will react with us. We need someone who will share our strong emotions. We need someone so involved that he will be afraid with us, be glad with us, be depressed with us; who will expose his own humanity as we expose ours. It is this contact between two human beings, revealing their common sensitivities, which draws them from loneliness and joins them together.

"Such sensitivity does not solve any problem or analyze any situation. Rather, it simply offers one human being the gift of another human being's self. It is an attempt to reach out and join hands with another person in this struggle which is life." [13]

LOVE IS . . .

Since you have been chosen by God who has given you this new kind of life, and because of his deep love and concern for you, you should practice tenderhearted mercy and kindness to others. Don't worry about making a good impression on them but be ready to·suffer quietly and patiently.

Colossians 3:12

Little children, let us stop just *saying* we love people; let us *really* love them, and *show* it by our *actions*.

1 John 3:18

Dear friends, let us practice loving each other, for love comes from God and those who are loving and kind show that they are the children of God, and that they are getting to know him better.

4:7

Don't just pretend that you love others: really love them. Hate what is wrong. Stand on the side of the good.

Romans 12:9

Love does no wrong to anyone. That's why it fully satisfies all of God's requirements. It is the only law you need.

13:10

But if a person isn't loving and kind, it shows that he doesn't know God—for God is love.

1 John 4:8

Be humble and gentle. Be patient with each other, making allowance for each other's faults because of your love.

Ephesians 4:2

In response to all he has done for us, let us outdo each other in being helpful and kind to each other and in doing good.

Hebrews 10:24

May God who gives patience, steadiness, and encouragement help you to live in complete harmony with each other—each with the attitude of Christ toward the other.

Romans 15:5

Try always to be led along together by the Holy Spirit, and so be at peace with one another.

Ephesians 4:3

Don't use bad language. Say only what is good and helpful to those you are talking to, and what will give them a blessing.

4:29

The Lord hates the thoughts of the wicked but delights in kind words.

Proverbs 15:26

So encourage each other to build each other up, just as you are already doing.

1 Thessalonians 5:11

1 Corinthians

13:4   Love is very patient and kind, never jealous or envious, never boastful or proud,

13:5   never haughty or selfish or rude. Love does not demand its own way. It is not irritable or touchy. It does not hold grudges and will hardly even notice when others do it wrong.

13:6   It is never glad about injustice, but rejoices whenever truth wins out.

13:7   If you love someone you will be loyal to him no matter what the cost. You will always believe in him, always expect the best of him, and always stand your ground in defending him.

Philippians 2:14   In everything you do, stay away from complaining and arguing.

CONSIDER THE NEEDS OF YOUR SPOUSE

Don't be selfish; don't live to make a good impression on others. Be humble, thinking of others as better than yourself.

Philippians 2:3

Don't just think about your own affairs, but be interested in others, too, and in what they are doing.

2:4

Now I want you to be leaders also in the spirit of cheerful giving . . . others are eager for it. This is one way to prove that your love is real, that it goes beyond mere words.

2 Corinthians 8:7, 8

Be gentle and ready to forgive; never hold grudges. Remember, the Lord forgave you, so you must forgive others.

Colossians 3:13

You wives, submit yourselves to your husbands. . . . And you husbands must be loving and kind to your wives and not bitter against them, nor harsh.

3:18, 19

EMPATHY

Galatians 6:2

Share each other's troubles and problems, and so obey our Lord's command.

Romans 12:15

When others are happy, be happy with them. If they are sad, share their sorrow.

1 Peter 3:8, 9

You should be like one big happy family, full of sympathy toward each other, loving one another with tender hearts and humble minds. Don't repay evil for evil. Don't snap back at those who say unkind things about you. Instead, pray for God's help for them, for we are to be kind to others, and God will bless us for it.

Philippians 2:2

Then make me truly happy by loving each other and agreeing wholeheartedly with each other, working together with one heart and mind and purpose.

COMMUNICATION

COMMUNICATION

"Communication is to love what blood is to the body." [1]

"All communication in an intimate relationship is built upon mutual trust. To confide in another is to be relatively sure, first of all, that a ground of confidence is shared. Mutual trust grows as each partner takes the other into account as a person whose happiness is bound up with his own." [2]

"If there is any indispensable insight with which a young married couple should begin their life together, it is that they should try to keep open, at all cost, the lines of communication between them." [3]

"Nothing communicates more readily than trust and concern for another's happiness. For an earnest Christian couple the basis for mutual trust is already established. And since they believe that God will bring forth His best in the face of human weakness, failure, and conflict, they dare to communicate openly and honestly with full acceptance of each other." [4]

"This is one way of saying that no amount of communication can make marriage perfect, and therefore we should not expect it. God is perfect, the ideal of Christian marriage is perfect, and the means God puts at the disposal of Christian couples are perfect. Yet there is no perfect marriage, no perfect communication in marriage. The glory of Christian marriage is in accepting the lifelong task of making continual adjustments within the disorder of human existence, ever working to improve communication skills necessary to this task, and seeking God's enabling power in it all." [5]

"Communication is essential to the expression of love and indeed to life itself. Where there is love, there must be communication, because love can never be passive and inactive. Love inevitably expresses itself and moves out toward others. When communication breaks down, love is blocked and its energy will turn to resentment and hostility." [6]

COMMUNICATION IS SHARING

"The art of marital communication is making it clear to your spouse, by word or touch or gesture, exactly what it is you mean by what you say, or exactly what emotions and attitudes underlie the words, inflections, and gestures. Used thus, communication can join two individuals in the psychic meshing of marital union." [7]

"Love is the opening of one's life to another in intimate, understanding communication. When two persons can share from the very center of their existence, they experience love in its truest quality. Marriage is a venture into intimacy, and intimacy is the opening of one self to another." [8]

"Communication never ends. What we are to one another cannot be silenced. What we say to each other by our words should resonate with our deeds, acts, and gifts to the other. Successful marriages are built by partners who achieve consistent communications both verbally and non-verbally. There will always be discrepancies. But they can be reduced to understandable minimums and overlooked in love if couples work at consistent communication and constant love." [9]

"Communication is the attempt on the part of two selves to find and to call each other out of the loneliness of independent selfhood into a relationship of mutual interest and purpose." [10]

ENJOY EACH OTHER BY BEING OPEN

"A marriage can be likened to a large house with many rooms to which a couple fall heir on their wedding day. Their hope is to use and enjoy these rooms, as we do the rooms in a comfortable home, so that they will serve the many activities that make up their shared life. But in many marriages, doors are found to be locked—they represent areas in the relationship which the couple are unable to explore together. Attempts to open these doors lead to failure and frustration. The right key cannot be found. So the couple resign themselves to living together in only a few rooms that can be opened easily, leaving the rest of the house, with all its promising possibilities, unexplored and unused.

"There is, however, a master key that will open every door. It is not easy to find. Or, more correctly, it has to be forged by the couple together, and this can be very difficult. It is the great art of effective marital communication." [11] *

"Without communication, the possibilities for a relationship become hopeless, the resources of the partners for the relationship are no longer available, the means for healing the hurts that previous communication may have caused are no longer present; and each, when he recovers from his need to justify himself and hurt the other, will find himself in a bottomless pit of loneliness from which he cannot be pulled except by the ropes of communication, which may or may not be capable of pulling him out again because of their weakened condition." [12]

* From *We Can Have Better Marriages if We Really Want Them* by David & Vera Mace. Copyright © 1974 by Abingdon Press. Used by permission.

BE CAREFUL OF YOUR SPEECH

James

1:26   Anyone who says he is a Christian but doesn't control his tongue is just fooling himself, and his religion isn't worth much.

3:2   If anyone can control his tongue, it proves that he has perfect control over himself in every other way.

3:5   So also the tongue is a small thing, but what enormous damage it can do. A great forest can be set on fire by one tiny spark.

3:6   And the tongue is a flame of fire. It is full of wickedness, and poisons every part of the body. And the tongue is set on fire by hell itself, and can turn our whole lives into a blazing flame of destruction and disaster.

3:7, 8   Men have trained, or can train, every kind of animal or bird that lives and every kind of reptile and fish, but no human being can tame the tongue. It is always ready to pour out its deadly poison.

3:9   Sometimes it praises our heavenly Father, and sometimes it breaks out into curses against men who are made like God.

3:10   And so blessing and cursing come pouring out of the same mouth. Dear brothers, surely this is not right!

THINK BEFORE YOU SPEAK

A wise man holds his tongue. Only a fool blurts out everything he knows; that only leads to sorrow and trouble.	Proverbs 10:14
A good man thinks before he speaks; the evil man pours out his evil words without a thought.	15:28
A man without self-control is as defenseless as a city with broken-down walls.	25:28
Self-control means controlling the tongue! A quick retort can ruin everything.	13:3
The man of few words and settled mind is wise; therefore, even a fool is thought to be wise when he is silent. It pays him to keep his mouth shut.	17:27, 28
Those who love to talk will suffer the consequences. Men have died for saying the wrong thing!	18:21

CHOOSE YOUR WORDS WISELY

Proverbs

12:18	Some people like to make cutting remarks, but the words of the wise soothe and heal.
15:4	Gentle words cause life and health; griping brings discouragement.
15:23	Everyone enjoys giving good advice, and how wonderful it is to be able to say the right thing at the right time!
16:24	Kind words are like honey—enjoyable and healthful.
18:4	A wise man's words express deep streams of thought.
25:11	Timely advice is as lovely as golden apples in a silver basket.
25:15	Be patient and you will finally win, for a soft tongue can break hard bones.
27:17	A friendly discussion is as stimulating as the sparks that fly when iron strikes iron.

A TIME TO SPEAK AND A TIME TO BE SILENT

Don't talk so much. You keep putting your foot in your mouth. Be sensible and turn off the flow!	Proverbs 10:19
Love forgets mistakes; nagging about them parts the best of friends.	17:9
A rebellious son is a calamity to his father, and a nagging wife annoys like constant dripping.	19:13
It is better to live in the corner of an attic than with a crabby woman in a lovely home.	21:9
Better to live in the desert than with a quarrelsome, complaining woman.	21:19
It is better to live in a corner of an attic than in a beautiful home with a cranky, quarrelsome woman.	25:24
A time to be quiet; a time to speak up.	Ecclesiastes 3:7

LISTENING

"How beautiful, how grand and liberating this experience is, when people learn to help each other. It is impossible to overemphasize the immense need humans have to be really listened to. Listen to all the conversations of our world, between nations as well as those between couples." [1]

"We can, if we are able to listen as well as to speak, become better informed and wiser as we grow older, instead of being stuck like some people with the same little bundle of prejudices at 65 that we had at 25." [2]

"If we would love, we must listen to one another. This is the first work of love. In listening we give ourselves to others. We give them our attention, we commit ourselves to them." [3]

"It is in listening that marriage matures." [4]

BE A CREATIVE LISTENER

"Creative listening is not passive but active; it communicates feelings of acceptance and need. It encourages the other person to analyze his own feelings and, miracle of miracles, to listen to himself. Creative listening involves empathy, the skill of being able to get into another person's skin, to discover his underlying motives, his emotional hungers. A little child was sent on an errand and was gone longer than her mother thought proper. When she returned and was asked for an explanation, she said, 'I met Mary and her doll was broken, so I stopped to help her.' 'You mean you helped her fix the doll?' her mother asked. 'No,' said the little girl, 'I stopped to help her cry.' Creative listening is to weep sincerely with your mate when he has been hurt, to enter into his pain and frustration, to penetrate his loneliness at its deepest level. As you share one another's joys and woes, power is released. Trouble has no opportunity to develop in this kind of environment." [5]

"Listening effectively means that when someone is talking you are not thinking about what you are going to say when the other person stops. Instead, you are totally tuned in to what the other person is saying." [6]

"The art of truly communicating with others—in marriage, or just in friendships—is the art of living richly, deeply, and with meaning. That calls for more than superficial interest in others. It demands caring. Caring enough to love. Caring enough to be understanding. Caring enough to listen to the other person. In normal daily friendships, listening is the first requirement of love." [7]

"Love is listening. Love is the opening of your life to another. Through sincere interest, simple attention, sensitive listening, compassionate understanding and honest sharing.

"An open ear is the only believable sign of an open heart. You learn to understand life—you learn to live—as you learn to listen.

"To love your neighbor is to listen to him as you listen to yourself. The golden rule of friendship—to listen to others as you would have them listen to you." [8]

THE ROAD TO MATURITY

"Listening brings about changes in people's attitudes towards themselves and others, and also brings about changes in their basic values and personal philosophy. People who have been listened to in this new and special way become more emotionally mature, more open to their experiences, less defensive, more democratic, and less authoritarian. When people are listened to sensitively, they tend to listen to themselves with more care and make clear exactly what they are feeling and thinking. Not the least important result of listening is the change that takes place within the listener himself." [9]

"By consistently listening to a speaker you are conveying the idea: 'I'm interested in you as a person; and I think that what you feel is important. I respect your thoughts, and even if I don't agree with them, I know that they are valid for you. I feel sure that you have a contribution to make. I'm not trying to change you or evaluate you. I just want to understand you. I think you're worth listening to, and I want you to know that I'm the kind of person that you can talk to.'" [10]

BE RESPONSIVE TO OTHERS BY LISTENING

"Listening is a sharp attention to what is going on. Listening is an active openness toward the other fellow. Listening is putting your whole self in a position to respond to whatever he cares to say." [11]

"If you listen you adventure in the lives of other people. We soon notice the people who really take us seriously and listen to what we have to say. And with them we tend to open more of our lives than with the busy nonlistener. We share what really matters. Thus, if you are such a listener, the chances are good that others will invite you as a guest into their lives. Because they know you will hear them, they will entrust you with things that mean very much to them. And this too is most rewarding!" [12]

"In some wonderful way that we can never fully understand, God too is a listener. In his listening, as in his speaking, he both loves and judges. He is both the Father and the Lord. Through our creative listening he acts in both ways. And where our listening is imperfect, he will find other ways of expressing his perfect love and judgment." [13]

IN LISTENING, LOVE MATURES

Proverbs

1:33	. . . all who listen to me shall live in peace and safety, unafraid.
8:33	Listen to my counsel—oh, don't refuse it—and be wise.
18:13	What a shame—yes, how stupid!—to decide before knowing the facts!
18:17	Any story sounds true until someone tells the other side and sets the record straight.
21:11	The wise man learns by listening; the simpleton can learn only by seeing scorners punished.
James 1:19	Dear brothers, don't ever forget that it is best to listen much, speak little, and not become angry.

LISTEN TO THE ADVICE OF YOUR SPOUSE

Pride leads to arguments; be humble, take advice and become wise.

Proverbs 13:10

If you refuse criticism you will end in poverty and disgrace; if you accept criticism you are on the road to fame.

13:18

If you profit from constructive criticism you will be elected to the wise men's hall of fame. But to reject criticism is to harm yourself and your own best interests.

15:31, 32

An evil man is stubborn, but a godly man will reconsider.

21:29

Don't refuse to accept criticism; get all the help you can.

23:12

It is a badge of honor to accept valid criticism.

25:12

A man who refuses to admit his mistakes can never be successful. But if he confesses and forsakes them, he gets another chance.

28:13

TRUTH

"The practice of honesty and clear communication in marriage is likely to result in an extra dividend, for it encourages spouses to be generous, comforting, and consoling. If the spouses can be truthful and open about themselves mutual support and helpfulness are possible." [1]

"Self-concealment may then be a way of lying. To shut off self-disclosure becomes a way of keeping up a false image. What may be a protective device at best, is at worst a lie. Concealment may be accomplished in a context of politeness, deference, even concern for the other person. But the motive is to deceive." [2]

"Honesty is part of love. A couple should be able to be honest about their thoughts, fears, deeds, motives, and desires. To live behind a mask is to deny one's partner the privilege of knowing his inner self. It also robs one of the power of a single-minded life." [3]

"Wise is the spouse who learns how to listen so as to make it easier for his mate to speak. The corollary of speaking the truth in love is hearing it. This may rule out quick rejoinders, and involve receiving one's partner's words in silence, with a caress, or with a meaningful but unspecific statement such as, 'The more I know you, the more I love you.'" [4]

"We can choose to give trust—if we really want to trust. Trust is love put in action. To love another is to be eager to trust, to extend that trust, to take risks in trusting." [5]

LET YOUR SOULS AND SPIRITS UNITE

"The great goal in marriage is complete openness and total intimacy of soul and spirit. This, however, does not happen overnight. It sometimes takes years to accomplish, and some couples never fully arrive. But God wants us to keep growing, each day exposing a little more of our souls to each other in Christian love and courtesy." [6]

"Because marriage is a relationship of shared intimacy, it requires a level of honesty between the partners that goes much deeper than conventional social relationships. People cannot truly share life without knowing each other, and they cannot know each other unless their thoughts are open to each other to a degree that happens in few other human relationships. To be secretive or reserved or defensive toward each other in marriage is inevitably to condemn the relationship to superficiality." [7] *

"The expression of true and honest feeling can be positive evidence that the family is secure enough to give us the freedom and ease to be ourselves even when those selves are irritated with one another. Such expression is dangerous only when the marriage is otherwise so fragile that it can be kept together only by superficial good manners. Such a family believes only in appearances, not in the God who is the source of its unity. It lives not by faith, but by fear." [8]

* From *We Can Have Better Marriages if We Really Want Them* by David & Vera Mace. Copyright © 1974 by Abingdon Press. Used by permission.

"It is not enough—it is never enough—to simply talk of telling the truth. A man can tell the truth and be a liar still. All he has to do is select what truths to tell, or which half-truths to combine, and with a smattering of skill and 'with a little bit of luck' he can be an 'honest' liar.

"It is not enough to talk of telling the truth or even of telling the whole truth.

"We must be the truth. Be true persons. Be truly human. Be true to self, be true to others and be true to God, the source of all truth.

"It's one thing to say the truth—it's another to be it.

"That's what makes Jesus Christ stand out." [9]

"What a release that is, to become a new, true person, to become the truth. And what a relief it is to be the truth. To be truly yourself before God, before others—and before yourself. No need to run and hide. No more games of hide-and-seek with your conscience. No more faking. No more playacting. No more false fronts or faces.

"You're free. Free to be the truth, the whole truth and nothing but the truth—by the help of God." [10]

"Truth with love brings healing. Truth told in love enables men to grow. Truth in love produces change. Truth and love are the two necessary ingredients for any relationship with integrity. Love—because all positive relationships begin with friendship, appreciation, respect. And truth—because no relationship of trust can long grow from dishonesty, deceit, betrayal; it springs up from the solid stuff of integrity." [11]

LOVE IS BUILT UPON TRUTH

Proverbs

10:18	To hate is to be a liar; to slander is to be a fool.
11:13	A gossip goes around spreading rumors, while a trustworthy man tries to quiet them.
12:13	Lies will get any man into trouble, but honesty is its own defense.
12:14	Telling the truth gives a man great satisfaction, and hard work returns many blessings to him.
12:17	A good man is known by his truthfulness; a false man by deceit and lies.
12:22	God delights in those who keep their promises, and abhors those who don't.
13:5	A good man hates lies; wicked men lie constantly and come to shame.
13:17	An unreliable messenger can cause a lot of trouble. Reliable communication permits progress.
25:18	Telling lies about someone is as harmful as hitting him with an axe, or wounding him with a sword, or shooting him with a sharp arrow.
Ephesians 4:25	Stop lying to each other; tell the truth, for we are parts of each other and when we lie to each other we are hurting ourselves.
Colossians 3:9	Don't tell lies to each other; it was your old life with all its wickedness that did that sort of thing; now it is dead and gone.
Ephesians 4:15, 16	Instead, we will lovingly follow the truth at all times—speaking truly, dealing truly, living truly—and so become more and more in every way like Christ who is the Head of his body, the church. Under his direction the whole body is fitted together perfectly, and each part in its own special way helps the other parts, so that the whole body is healthy and growing and full of love.

FLATTERY OR FRANKNESS?

It is an honor to receive a frank reply.   Proverbs 24:26

Pretty words may hide a wicked heart, just as a pretty glaze   26:23
covers a common clay pot.

Flattery is a form of hatred and wounds cruelly.   26:28

In the end, people appreciate frankness more than flattery.   28:23

Their tongues are filled with flatteries to gain their wicked   Psalms 5:9, 10
ends. . . . they rebel against you.

Don't insist that I be cautious lest I insult someone, and   Job 32:22
don't make me flatter anyone. Let me be frank, lest God
should strike me dead.

HUMILITY BUILDS RELATIONSHIPS

Proverbs

15:33   Humility and reverence for the Lord will make you both wise and honored.

17:19   Sinners love to fight; boasting is looking for trouble.

18:12   Pride ends in destruction; humility ends in honor.

27:2   Don't praise yourself; let others do it!

Luke 14:11   For everyone who tries to honor himself shall be humbled; and he who humbles himself shall be honored.

Colossians 3:12   Since you have been chosen by God who has given you this new kind of life, and because of his deep love and concern for you, you should practice tenderhearted mercy and kindness to others. Don't worry about making a good impression on them but be ready to suffer quietly and patiently.

UNDERSTANDING

"You well know that beautiful prayer of Francis of Assisi: 'Lord! Grant that I may seek more to understand than to be understood. . . .' It is this new desire which the Holy Spirit awakens in couples and which transforms their marriage. As long as a man is preoccupied primarily with being understood by his wife, he is miserable, overcome with self-pity, the spirit of demanding, and bitter withdrawal. As soon as he becomes preoccupied with understanding her, seeking to understand that which he had not before understood, and with his own wrongdoing in not having understood her, then the direction taken by events begins to change. As soon as a person feels understood, he opens up, and because he lowers his defenses he is also able to make himself better understood." [1]

UNDERSTAND THE GIFTS OF GOD

"Differentness is another way of saying 'individuality.' We were created as irreplaceable individuals, different from any who have gone before or who will appear again. This is a frightening thought to insecure people who have not realized that God considers each person to be a talented individual of unique worth." [2]

"Yes, every good happening is of God, a gift of God. Every deliverance from loneliness, fear, suffering, or remorse is a result of the loving mercy of God. This is so even if neither the recipient nor the instrument recognize it, and take all the credit themselves.

"Happy are the couples who do recognize and understand that their happiness is a gift of God, who can kneel together to express their thanks not only for the love which he brings about through that hard school of mutual understanding." [3]

"To find the key to understanding, the secret of living—this is an inner experience, a discovery, a conversion, and not simply an acquisition of new knowledge. It may happen at the very time when a person feels most disheartened; it generally takes place in a way which he could not have imagined. He may have read many books, heard many sermons, accumulated much knowledge. And yet suddenly, it is a rather insignificant happening which strikes him, a word, an encounter, a death, a recovery, a look, or a natural event. God uses such to reach a man." [4]

CONFLICT CAN BRING UNDERSTANDING

"You would observe that well upstream, before they united, each river flowed gently along. But right at the point of their union, look out!

"Those two nice streams came at each other like fury. I have actually seen them on days when it was almost frightening to watch. They clashed in a wild commotion of frenzy and confusion. They hurled themselves head on as if each was determined that the other should end its existence right there.

"Then, as you watched, you could almost see the angry white caps pair off, bow in respect to each other, and join forces as if to say 'Let us get along now. Ahead of us there is something better.'

"Sure enough, on downstream, at some distance, the river swept steadily on once more. It was broader there, more majestic, and it gave you the feeling that something good had been fashioned out of the conflict.

"A good marriage is often like that. When two independent streams of existence come together, there will probably be some dashing of life against life at the juncture. Personalities rush against each other. Preferences clash. Ideas contend for power and habits vie for position. Sometimes, like the waves, they throw up a spray that leaves you breathless and makes you wonder where has the loveliness gone.

"But that's all right. Like the two rivers, what comes out of their struggle may be something deeper, more powerful than what they were on their own." [5]

CONTRAST IN VIEWS CAN BE AN ASSET

"Marriage introduces a world full of pictures. The selection of a mate is marked by many dreams and wishes. We have our ideas, our conceptions about marriage, about our mate—ideas which we've inherited or collected and which fill us with anticipation. The success or failure of a marriage often depends upon the ability to survive disappointments or to refashion our dreams to fit reality." [6]

"Every marriage is like a set of fingerprints with its own unique pattern. Each spouse begins with certain ideas and preferences that may be subject to the influence or pressure of the other. To have an opinion, to believe in something, is natural to all of us. But we need to be flexible, for our personal views may not be the right or the only ones.

"We must accept difference, even to the point of understanding that what seems to be an infuriating contrast in views can ultimately be an asset." [7]

"An accepting attitude permits the spouse to maintain his self-respect, and acknowledges that at some points he has probably made courageous attempts to improve the marriage, that he may have been greatly influenced by his family background, and that the accepting spouse is also human, and therefore imperfect. Acceptance stresses greater understanding and empathy—the forerunners of genuine forgiveness." [8]

UNDERSTANDING

Be humble and gentle. Be patient with each other, making allowance for each other's faults because of your love.

Ephesians 4:2

Can't you hear the voice of wisdom? She is standing at the city gates. . . . Listen to what she says: . . . Let me give you understanding. O foolish ones, let me show you common sense!

Proverbs 8:1-5

Men with common sense are admired as counselors.

10:13

Love is very patient and kind, never jealous or envious, never boastful or proud, never haughty or selfish or rude. If you love someone you will be loyal to him no matter what the cost.

1 Corinthians 13:4, 7

SEX

"The sexual bond is the gift of the supreme secret, supreme intimacy, of the finest, most personal secret, one's own body. . . . There is inscribed in the human soul a law of all or nothing in love. The gift of one's body is only the sign of this decision to make a complete gift of self which will imply also the mutual gift of all one's secrets. . . . When you love and feel yourself loved you can express yourself. You discover yourself by expressing yourself, at the same time that you discover the other partner." [1]

"Sex is a God-ordained means of assuring your partner that he is the most important person in the world right here, right now." [2]

THERE IS POETRY IN SEX

KING SOLOMON: "How beautiful you are, my love, how beautiful! Your eyes are those of doves. Your hair falls across your face like flocks of goats that frisk across the slopes of Gilead. Your teeth are white as sheep's wool, newly shorn and washed; perfectly matched, without one missing. Your lips are like a thread of scarlet—and how beautiful your mouth. Your cheeks are matched loveliness behind your locks. Your neck is stately as the tower of David, jeweled with a thousand heroes' shields. Your breasts are like twin fawns of a gazelle, feeding among the lilies. Until the morning dawns and the shadows flee away, I will go to the mountain of myrrh and to the hill of frankincense. You are so beautiful, my love, in every part of you.

"Come with me from Lebanon, my bride. We will look down from the summit of the mountain, from the top of Mount Hermon, where the lions have their dens, and panthers prowl. You have ravished my heart, my lovely one, my bride; I am overcome by one glance of your eyes, by a single bead of your necklace. How sweet is your love, my darling, my bride. How much better it is than mere wine. The perfume of your love is more fragrant than all the richest spices. Your lips, my dear, are made of honey. Yes, honey and cream are under your tongue, and the scent of your garments is like the scent of the mountains and cedars of Lebanon.

"My darling bride is like a private garden, a spring that no one else can have, a fountain of my own. You are like a lovely orchard bearing precious fruit, with the rarest of perfumes; nard and saffron, calamus and cinnamon, and perfume from every other incense tree, as well as myrrh and aloes, and every other lovely spice. You are a garden fountain, a well of living water, refreshing as the streams from the Lebanon mountains."

Song of Solomon 4:1-15

CELEBRATE THROUGH SEXUALITY

"Sex is celebration of creation.

"As created people we do not exist as individuals. We are not meant to be individuals. We are persons. We are designed for relationship, incomplete in isolation. We cannot recognize ourselves without others; we cannot truly know ourselves except in relation to another. Sex is a celebration of God's dual creation, man-woman.

"Sexuality is also our celebration of God's continuing creativity. God has chosen to mediate His creative activity in the conception of new persons through the intimate act of love-union. He has honored the simple act of joining bodies with the ultimate significance of beginning life.

"Two who give themselves to each other in the intimacy of marriage, celebrate the eternal potential of their act of love. This awareness of its creative meaning gives character to sexual union even when it is meant as an act of joyous communion with no intention of conception. Then, too, it is a celebration of His creation." [3]

MATURITY BEGINS WITH SHARING

"Sex plays a special part in the sharing of God's love. God transmits the meaning of love to us through other people, and uniquely through families. When a husband and wife manifest in their marital relations a humble faith in God and are renewed daily by an awareness of the indwelling Christ, they are able to fulfill each other in a way that overcomes their emptiness. Their mutual love gives them a confidence that they are accepted in life and have a belonging in eternity. This is the essence of salvation—and the beginning of maturity!

"This religious dimension allows them to accept one another as persons and not 'things.' It frees them for creative living in the relaxed atmosphere of a home where both can develop their own personalities without domination. There is a mutual concern for one another and a striving for shared goals." [4]

But usually it is best to be married, each man having his own wife, and each woman having her own husband, because otherwise you might fall back into sin.

1 Corinthians 7:2

The man should give his wife all that is her right as a married woman, and the wife should do the same for her husband:

7:3

for a girl who marries no longer has full right to her own body, for her husband then has his rights to it, too; and in the same way the husband no longer has full right to his own body, for it belongs also to his wife.

7:4

So do not refuse these rights to each other. The only exception to this rule would be the agreement of both husband and wife to refrain from the rights of marriage for a limited time, so that they can give themselves more completely to prayer. Afterwards, they should come together again so that Satan won't be able to tempt them because of their lack of self-control.

7:5

Honor your marriage and its vows, and be pure; for God will surely punish all those who are immoral or commit adultery.

Hebrews 13:4

FORGIVENESS

FORGIVENESS

"Forgive, and forget the past. Dwelling on past hurts, bringing up past faults, or limiting one's present acts by expecting a repetition of past behavior only builds up emotional barriers. How easy it is to 'imprison' your partner mentally in a certain pattern of behavior, thereby condemning him to remain unchanged. Our faith is in a God who can and does work miracles, both in ourselves and in others.

"In prayer, forgive your spouse for whatever has happened. Go even further and accept responsibility for all the misunderstandings that have grown up between the two of you. Needless to say, your partner cannot receive your forgiveness unless he repents. God forgives you, even before you sin, so practice forgiveness toward your spouse regardless of attitudes you may feel justified in expecting from him." [1]

FORGIVENESS TAKES SERIOUS THOUGHT

"Real forgiveness costs; it hurts. He who forgives, gives himself for the other in spite of hurt and sin. He regards the act with dead seriousness. He does not make light of the sin or say that it does not matter. If one can talk lightly of forgiveness he is not forgiving; he is condoning something that he does not take seriously. When we love one whom we know has hurt another and himself and God, we are tempted to excuse rather than forgive. It is impossible to be forgiving without acknowledging both the seriousness of sin and our involvement in it, and the forgiveness of God for both ourselves and the other.

"Christ went to the depths of suffering in his forgiveness. No one saw so clearly how we hurt one another and God. Yet, through the cross, bearing the pain of our self-centeredness, he made it possible for us to be forgiven. To realize his cost enables us to bear the cost of forgiving one another. It will continue to cost us. God's forgiveness restores those who are alienated. It does not take away the fact of sin or its consequences. It does not take away the memory of sin; the Prodigal would never forget his exploits in the far country. God reestablishes the relationship which has been broken by our sin. When we experience this reconciliation, we are able to share it with those who are separated from us." [2]

FORGIVENESS IS NOT A BARGAIN

"Forgiveness is not the same as tolerance. Tolerating an evil action is possible where there is moral neutrality—either weakness or insensitivity to the nature of the evil.

"Forgiveness is not leniency. It is not merely a soft attitude toward a harsh fact.

"Forgiveness is not condescension. A husband or wife cannot effectively reconcile the other by condescending.

"Forgiveness does not demand guarantees. Less than true forgiveness is offered whenever a husband or wife says to the other, 'I'll forgive you if you promise never to do that again.' That is conditional forgiveness—a deal!—but the forgiveness of which the New Testament speaks is never equated with driving a bargain. Christian forgiveness risks the future; it gives and risks all!

"Forgiveness has nothing to do with justice. If a person is determined to stand on his rights, he will not forgive—he can't forgive.

"Forgiveness is an empathic, felt event. We feel genuine forgiveness, whether we're the one forgiving or forgiven. As one who receives forgiveness, we first feel the pain of what it is that must be forgiven. We feel the humiliation of our need for forgiveness, of having to be forgiven by one we've hurt." [3]

THE CHRISTIAN FORGIVES AND FORGETS

"How often do I need forgiveness? I will have many opportunities every day to ask for forgiveness. The more closely I look to Jesus and react to Him, the more clearly I note how often my words or even my thoughts are contrary to His will." [4] *

"Maturity in marriage means being able to forgive and forget. To a Christian this power is at the very core of his experience. He has been loved, accepted, and forgiven by God, and this is his greatest gift. Because of it he can face the future fearlessly with joy and gladness and, without undue anxiety, can forgive others. Not that such action is easy from a human standpoint, but it was not easy for God either—it cost him his Son on a cross." [5]

"Forgiveness is hard. Especially in a marriage tense with past troubles, tormented by fears of rejection and humiliation, and torn by suspicion and distrust.

"Forgiveness hurts. Especially when it must be extended to a husband or wife who doesn't deserve it, who hasn't earned it, who may misuse it. It hurts to forgive.

"Forgiveness costs. Especially in marriage when it means accepting instead of demanding repayment for the wrong done; where it means releasing the other instead of exacting revenge; where it means reaching out in love instead of relishing resentments. It costs to forgive." [6]

---

* From *Love in Action* by Wilhard Becker, Copyright © 1969 by Zondervan Publishing House and used by permission.

FORGIVENESS BRINGS LOVE, NOT HATRED

"Forgiving is self-giving with no self-seeking. It gives love where the enemy expects hatred. It gives freedom where the enemy deserves punishment. It gives understanding where the enemy anticipates anger and revenge. Forgiveness refuses to seek its own advantage. It gives back to the other person his freedom and his future." [7]

"When I have received forgiveness myself from Jesus, then I can forgive. And here the circuit of love is closed. This is also the secret of answered prayer: 'And whenever you stand praying, forgive, if you have anything against any one; so that your Father also who is in heaven may forgive you your trespasses.'" [8] *

"Forgiveness is the key to love. Perhaps this seems surprising and hard to understand, but Jesus Himself states the principle in Luke 7:47—the more forgiveness, the more love. But forgiveness requires capitulation. Only when I recognize and confess my own inability and my failure does God forgive, that is, does His forgiveness become effective." [9] *

"An apology is so often considered a sign of weakness, whereas in reality it is a sign of strength. It is more difficult, sometimes, to confess our weaknesses or to parade our faults in the face of those whom we most dearly love than in the presence of anyone else. This may be a recoiling from any chance of destroying the other's respect for us. It may also simply be ego in its proudest parade." [10]

FORGIVENESS AND CONFESSION ARE ESSENTIALS IN MARRIAGE

Ephesians 4:32	Instead, be kind to each other, tenderhearted, forgiving one another, just as God has forgiven you because you belong to Christ.
Colossians 3:13	Be gentle and ready to forgive; never hold grudges. Remember, the Lord forgave you, so you must forgive others.
Matthew 6:14, 15	Your heavenly Father will forgive you if you forgive those who sin against you; but if *you* refuse to forgive *them, he* will not forgive *you.*
James 5:16	Admit your faults to one another and pray for each other so that you may be healed. The earnest prayer of a righteous man has great power and wonderful results.
1 Peter 2:1	So get rid of your feelings of hatred. Don't just pretend to be good! Be done with dishonesty and jealousy and talking about others behind their backs.
1 Peter 4:8	Most important of all, continue to show deep love for each other, for love makes up for many of your faults.
Proverbs 17:9	Love forgets mistakes.

86

LOVE AND FORGIVENESS

Hatred stirs old quarrels, but love overlooks insults.   Proverbs 10:12

A fool is quick-tempered; a wise man stays cool when   12:16
insulted.

If you repay evil for good, a curse is upon your home.   17:13

Don't repay evil for evil. Wait for the Lord to handle   20:22
the matter.

Never pay back evil for evil. Do things in such a way   Romans 12:17
that everyone can see you are honest clear through.

Dear friends, never avenge yourselves. Leave that to God,   12:19
for he has said that he will repay those who deserve it.

This suffering is all part of the work God has given you.   1 Peter 2:21
Christ, who suffered for you, is your example. Follow in
his steps.

He never sinned, never told a lie,   2:22

never answered back when insulted; when he suffered   2:23
he did not threaten to get even; he left his case in the
hands of God who always judges fairly.

CRITICISM

"But in spite of the difficulty it is possible to reform, to remake your husband or wife, if you know where to begin, how to proceed, and what to change. Where shall you begin?

"With yourself. Begin with you. Before you can have any hope of changing your partner you will need to make some very crucial changes. Since criticizing and suggesting changes only increase resistance—consciously or unconsciously—and since prodding and pushing only increase the problem by decreasing understanding, love and acceptance between you, discard it. Stop it all. Determine to give the most wholehearted love and acceptance possible. Without conditions. But then, if you can't criticize and correct the other, how will you proceed? By being a different sort of person. Instead of accepting with spoken or unspoken reservations, genuinely accept him or her as you promised in that long ago ceremony. Vows are nothing if they do not become a way of life—a daily commitment of life. And your vows were not to educate, reform and restructure your mate, but to love. The crucial commitment of marriage is the pledge to be the right mate to the other person. Forget whether you 'found the right mate.' Who could know? Who could say? And so what if you did or didn't discover just-the-very-very-right-and-perfect-person-for-grand-old-you?

"What kind of person are you being? Are you committed to being the right mate here and now? Do that, be that, and you'll make a change for the better in both of you. Almost instantly." [1]

"But at root it is our inability to accept each other as we really are that sabotages our marriages. Where criticism is a commodity and forgiveness is in short supply, you have a ready market for marital disaster." [2]

CHANGE YOURSELF BEFORE
CHANGING OTHERS

"Don't criticize, and then you won't be criticized. For others will treat you as you treat them. And why worry about a speck in the eye of a brother when you have a board in your own? Should you say, 'Friend, let me help you get that speck out of your eye,' when you can't even see because of the board in your own? Hypocrite! First get rid of the board. Then you can see to help your brother" (Matthew 7:1-5).

FORGET CRITICISM AND FORGIVE

"Every person should have a special cemetery lot in which to bury the faults of friends and loved ones." [3]

"The happiest people are less forgetting and more forgiving." [4]

"The best way to get even is to forget." [5]

"When a compliment and criticism are given in the same breath, the person will hear only the criticism." [6]

"It is much easier to be critical than to be correct." [7]

"I find the pain of a little censure, even when it is unfounded, is more acute than the pleasure of much praise." [8]

CRITICS ARE NOT SYMPATHETIC

"Criticizing another rarely gives us a valid insight into life and living. Certainly criticism inspires feelings, but they're feelings of superiority, not sympathy. No, in most critical comments about people, there's more enmity than empathy." [9]

"We criticize because it does something for us. Something we're not willing to name and face, but something that makes us feel good— for the moment.

"Which should reveal to us that chronic, critical attitudes are actually symptoms of emotional disturbance. The knocker, complainer, belittler or gossiper is sick. People who make trouble are generally troubled people.

"People pick at others to salve their own feelings of guilt by pointing out others who are worse than they.

"Or to scapegoat others for faults they find difficult to own up to in themselves.

"Or to ease emotional tensions and frustrations within their own personalities.

"Or to fulfill their own wishes and desires in imagination since they cannot or will not do them in act." [10]

IT TAKES TWO TO CRITICIZE

"Criticism can be a moral problem for both the talker and the listener. It takes two to backbite. The listener is just as guilty as the speaker. No real man can stand by while an absent and likely innocent person is dirtied. It is a human responsibility to protest the smearing of a fellow human. Why not gently say, 'I'd rather not listen to the criticism of another when he's not present to defend himself.' Or ask, 'Why do you think I should be told this story about him?'

"If you know something that would hurt or hinder the life or reputation of another, bury it. Forget it. End it right there. It will rest in peace. So will you.

"Love can even remove a beam of malice from a critical eye.

"Love heals. Love encourages. Love protects. Love looks for the best in others so that others may be their best." [11]

JUDGE WITH COMPASSION AND LOVE

"But there are times when a man must judge. What then?

"He must judge and criticize lovingly—for the purpose of helping, lifting and redeeming. Not to punish or get even.

"He must judge honestly, admitting where he too is guilty of the same fault and dealing as severely with himself as with others.

"He must criticize humbly, realizing that his own life is open to the scrutiny of the Judge of all the earth.

"Only when a man attempts to judge in honesty, in humility and in charity is his own eye clear. Only then is the plank of an unloving, malicious or vengeful spirit removed. Only then is the beam of his own sinful actions and attitudes withdrawn. Then he can see his way clear to remove the splinter in the other's eye. Not to label it and give his brother a sore eye. But to offer the hand of help. And healing.

"That's accepting others as persons, treating them as fellow human beings in need of the mercy and love of God. And demonstrating forgiveness even in criticism.

"Don't we owe them the loving, understanding, forgiving help as one all-too-human being to another?

"After all, that's the kind of merciful, compassionate love God showed us in Jesus Christ. And Jesus Christ gives that same strength to love and forgive to all those who open their lives to Him, risking the label 'Christian' to follow Him daily in life." [12]

CRITICISM BRINGS DISCOURAGEMENT

But if instead of showing love among yourselves you are always critical and catty, watch out! Beware of ruining each other.

Galatians 5:15

So don't criticize each other any more. Try instead to live in such a way that you will never make your brother stumble by letting him see you doing something he thinks is wrong.

Romans 14:13

So encourage each other to build each other up, just as you are already doing.

1 Thessalonians 5:11

ANGER

61464

"Do not talk when angry but after you have calmed down, do talk. Sometimes we push each other away and the problem between us festers. Just as in surgery free and adequate drainage is essential if healing is to take place."[1]

"1. Be angry, but beware—you are never more vulnerable than when in anger. Self-control is at an all-time low, reason decreases, common sense usually forsakes you.

2. Be angry, but be aware—that anger quickly turns bitter, it sours into resentment, hatred, malice, evil temper and even violence unless it is controlled by love.

3. Be angry, but only to be kind. Only when anger is motivated by love of your brother, by love of what is right for people, by what is called from you by love for God, is it constructive, creative anger."[2]

DON'T IGNORE ANGRY FEELINGS; CONTROL THEM

"As a Christian you may honestly think that because you know Christ you are not supposed to become angry—the anger is not a legitimate emotion for you. Therefore, when angry feelings arise you attempt to ignore them and refuse to accept their presence. Because of what you've been taught in sermons and possibly in things that you have read, you feel that anger is always a sin and therefore off limits for anyone practicing Christian behavior.

"But this isn't the case and it isn't what Scripture actually teaches. Anger is a God-given emotion. The Bible doesn't teach us to repress anger but to control it. In a way, we need anger as part of our personality and makeup.

"As Dr. J. H. Jowett says, 'A life incapable of anger is destitute of the needful energy for all reform. There is no blaze in it, there is no ministry of purification. . . . We are taught in the New Testament that this power of indignation is begotten by the Holy Spirit. The Holy Spirit makes us capable of healthy heat, and it inspires the fire within us. The Holy Spirit doesn't create a character that is lukewarm, neutral or indifferent.'" [3]

"Explosive anger is 'the curse of interpersonal relations.' Vented anger may ventilate feelings and provide instant, though temporary, release for tortured emotions, but it does little for relationships.

"Clearly expressed anger is something different. Clear statements of angry feelings and angry demands can slice through emotional barriers or communications tangles and establish contact." [4]

ANGER CAN BE CONSTRUCTIVE

"Jesus Christ experienced anger in his life, and for a very good reason.

"The gospel records make it perfectly plain that he could on occasion feel blazing anger and, feeling it, could and did give emphatic expression to it. For example, in Mark, chapter 3, the story is told of his healing on the Sabbath a man with a withered hand. When some protested that it was altogether improper to heal a man on the Sabbath, Jesus was indignant at their stubbornly perverted sense of values. The Scripture says that he 'looked round about on them with anger, being grieved for the hardness of their hearts.' In Matthew 23, the account is given of Jesus' blasting the scribes and Pharisees, whom he describes as 'hypocrites' for the revolting contrast between their high religious profession and their low irreligious practices. And in John 2 it is recorded that Jesus cleansed the Temple of its money-changers, insisting that his Father's house must not be made a house of merchandise." [4]

Jesus felt free to be angry and to let it show and to express it clearly.

It should be obvious from these illustrations that anger is not necessarily bad. But the results of anger can be either constructive or destructive, positive or negative.

Anger is a force, a gunpowder which, depending upon how it is directed, can blast away at wrong or can be used for wrong itself.

LET LOVE GUIDE YOUR ANGER

"Anger is a positive emotion, a self-affirming emotion which responds reflexively to the threat of rejection or devaluation with the messages (1) I am a person, a precious person and (2) I demand that you recognize and respect me.

"The energies of anger can flow in self-affirming ways when directed by love—the awareness of the other person's equal preciousness.

"Anger energies become a creative force when they are employed (1) to change my own behavior which ignored the other's preciousness and (2) to confront the other with his or her need to change unloving behavior. Anger energy can be directed at the cause of the anger, to get at the demands I am making, to own them, and then either correct my demanding self by canceling the demand, or call on the other to hear my demand and respond to how I see our relationship and what I want." [5]

THE CHRISTIAN SHOULD FEEL
RIGHTEOUS ANGER

The Scriptures not only permit anger but on some occasions *demand it!* Perhaps this sounds strange to some who have thought for years that anger is all wrong. But the Word of God states that we *are to be angry!*

"This, then, immediately disposes of the idea that the meek are passive persons who never get angry. There is no passivity in meekness. When the Lord Jesus Christ comes into our hearts, He does not go to sleep and put us to sleep. He becomes aggressively active within us.

". . . a Christian does and should get angry. But he must be careful to get angry at the right things and refrain from getting angry at the wrong things. Before he was saved and became blessed, his anger was sinful. Now it must be righteous. Meekness is the sanctification of anger." [6]

HATE THE SIN; LOVE THE SINNER

"Righteous anger is not sinful when it is properly directed. Such anger is an abiding settled attitude of righteous indignation against sin and sinful things coupled with appropriate action.

"There are several characteristics of righteous anger. First of all it must be controlled, not a heated, uncontrollable passion. Even if the cause is legitimate and is directed at an injustice, uncontrolled anger can make great error in judgment and increase the difficulty. The mind must be in control of the emotions so that the ability to reason is not lost. 'Be angry and sin not.'

"Second, there must be no hatred, malice or resentment. Anger that harbors a counter attack only complicates the problem. Jesus' reaction to the injustices delivered against Him is a good example. 'When He was reviled and insulted, He did not revile or offer insult in return; when He was abused and suffered, He made no threats of vengeance; but He trusted Himself and everything to Him who judges fairly' (*see* 1 Peter 2:23). 'Beloved, never avenge yourselves, but leave the way open for God's wrath: for it is written, Vengeance is mine, I will repay, says the Lord' (*see* Romans 12:19).

"A third characteristic of righteous anger is that its motivation is unselfish. When the motivation is selfish, usually resentment and pride are involved. Anger should be directed not at wrong done to oneself but at injustice done to others.

"Another characteristic of righteous anger is that it is directed against wrong things, deeds, or situations, not against people. Jesus said that we are to love all people. He excludes no one. We can hate the sin and be angry at it, but we must love the sinner." [7]

ADMIT AND CONFESS YOUR ANGER

"The final method of dealing with anger is to *confess* it. This is perhaps the best method, especially if it is coupled with an intelligent and healthy use of suppression or self-control. Confess the fact that you are angry—to yourself, to God, and to the person involved. Don't say, 'You're making me angry.' The individual is not making you angry. You are responsible for your own emotional reaction toward him. You could say, 'The way our discussion is going I'm getting angry. I'm not sure that's the best reaction so perhaps we could start over in our discussion.' Or, 'I'm sorry but I'm angry. What can I do now so we can resolve our differences?' Try admitting and confessing your anger.

"James suggests that we confess our faults to one another. This *does not mean* that all of our anger is sinful or wrong! Just the admission of being angry can help you release the feeling and get the message across in an acceptable manner to the person involved." [8]

WHAT DOES ANGER DO FOR YOUR MARRIAGE?

Proverbs

11:29	The fool who provokes his family to anger and resentment will finally have nothing worthwhile left. He shall be the servant of a wiser man.
14:17	A short-tempered man is a fool. He hates the man who is patient.
15:18	A quick-tempered man starts fights; a cool-tempered man tries to stop them.
16:32	It is better to be slow-tempered than famous; it is better to have self-control than to control an army.
18:6, 7	A fool gets into constant fights. His mouth is his undoing! His words endanger him.
19:19	A short-tempered man must bear his own penalty; you can't do much to help him. If you try once you must try a dozen times!
22:24, 25	Keep away from angry, short-tempered men, least you learn to be like them and endanger your soul.
29:20	There is more hope for a fool than for a man of quick temper.
29:8	Fools start fights everywhere while wise men try to keep peace.
29:9	There's no use arguing with a fool. He only rages and scoffs, and tempers flare.
29:11	A rebel shouts in anger; a wise man holds his temper in and cools it.
29:22	A hot-tempered man starts fights and gets into all kinds of trouble.
Ephesians 4:26, 27	If you are angry, don't sin by nursing your grudge. Don't let the sun go down with you still angry—get over it quickly; for when you are angry you give a mighty foothold to the devil.
James 1:20	for anger doesn't make us good, as God demands that we must be.

108

DISAGREEMENTS

DISAGREEMENTS

"As a reality in marriage, conflict can be creatively managed for good; it is part of the growth process. Don't ever underestimate its positive possibilities!" [1]

"In Christian marriage, conflict—with its demand for confession, forgiveness, and reconciliation—is a means God employs to teach humility." [2]

DIFFERENCES LEAD TO MARITAL CONFLICT

"So let us look more closely at marital conflict. Marriage is the coming together of two unique and different individuals in order to share life with each other. Their differences are quite unavoidable. They have lived separate lives for perhaps twenty to twenty-five years, during which each has developed a set of individual tastes, preferences, habits, likes and dislikes, values and standards. It is totally unreasonable to suppose that two people, just because they are married to each other, should always want to do the same thing in the same way at the same time.

"This doesn't happen even with identical twins. So the couple have differences of opinion and of choice, and these differences lead to disagreements. The couple may be quite willing to do the same thing in the same way, but at different times; or to do the same thing at the same time, but in different ways. How do they solve this problem? Either they must give up the idea altogether, and both feel frustrated and blame each other; or one will have to give up his particular wish and do it in the way, or at the time, the other wishes. People in love are able to do a good deal of giving up and giving in because love creates a generous mood. But sooner or later a situation develops in which neither is willing to accommodate the other because patience is exhausted, or enough ground has already been surrendered, or this time it is a matter of principle. So they are deadlocked, and now we have a conflict.

"What exactly *is* marital conflict? It is a disagreement, a state of opposed wills, that has been *heated up by emotion*—anger, resentment, hurt feelings, anxiety. The emotion is caused by frustration because you want or need something and you can't get it.

"What then is a disagreement which starts a conflict? It is a situation created by difference—two people with different wishes or objectives confront each other and are temporarily deadlocked." [3] *

* From *We Can Have Better Marriages if We Really Want Them* by David & Vera Mace. Copyright © 1974 by Abingdon Press. Used by permission.

"Disagreements are inevitable at many points in marriage and family living. Sometimes spouses become competitors as well as helpers and complements to one another. Rather than the isolation and alienation which accompanies conflict too often in the home, couples need to overcome the loneliness, to reduce the personal hurt, retaliation and recrimination. To accomplish this, differences must be brought out into the open so that good communication can be restored. Angry reactions are inevitable in a person's life, especially in the closeness and intimacy of family life, but the most important consideration is what one does with anger." [4] *

CONFLICT CAN BE POSITIVE

"The most frequent conflicts husbands and wives experience are verbal. Verbal conflict in itself is not harmful; any damage it causes depends upon the maturity of the two people in conflict. Entirely different ends can be served by a verbal clash, and some of them are healthy and good. Conflict can open doors of communication as well as shut them. As a reality in marriage, conflict can be creatively managed for good; it is part of the growth process. Don't ever underestimate its positive possibilties!" [5]

"Disagreements come and they must be handled in one way or another; quarreling is one way and necessary at times. We must also make the distinction that *disagreements* are one thing, *behaving disagreeably* is quite another." [6]

"A Christian response to disagreements includes a willingness to be patient in working out a solution.

"The willingness to exchange information, feelings, and ideas with one another leads to mutual understanding. Our first idea about a problem will not always be the same as our later understandings of it. As new ideas are expressed and the discussion develops, the issues may change." [7]

WILL QUARRELING BUILD
YOUR MARRIAGE?

To quarrel with a neighbor is foolish; a man with good sense holds his tongue.	Proverbs 11:12
A soft answer turns away wrath, but harsh words cause quarrels.	15:1
It is hard to stop a quarrel once it starts, so don't let it begin.	17:14
A quarrelsome man starts fights as easily as a match sets fire to paper.	26:21
Don't quarrel with anyone. Be at peace with everyone, just as much as possible.	Romans 12:18
Stop being mean, bad-tempered and angry. Quarreling, harsh words, and dislike of others should have no place in your lives.	Ephesians 4:31
Try to stay out of all quarrels and seek to live a clean and holy life, for one who is not holy will not see the Lord.	Hebrews 12:14

PRAYER

"It is only when a husband and wife pray together before God that they find the secret of true harmony, that the difference in their temperaments, their ideas, and their tastes enriches their home instead of endangering it. There will be no further question of one imposing his will on the other, or of the other giving in for the sake of peace. Instead, they will together seek God's will, which alone will ensure that each will be fully able to develop his personality. . . . When each of the marriage partners seeks quietly before God to see his own faults, recognizes his sin, and asks the forgiveness of the other, marital problems are no more. Each learns to speak the other's language, and to meet him halfway, so to speak. Each holds back those harsh little words which one is apt to utter when one is right, but which are said in order to injure. Most of all, a couple rediscovers complete mutual confidence, because, in meditating in prayer together, they learn to become absolutely honest with each other. . . . This is the price to be paid if partners very different from each other are to combine their gifts instead of setting them against each other." [1]

"Lines open to God are invariably open to one another for a person cannot be genuinely open to God and closed to his mate. Praying together especially reduces the sense of competitiveness in marriage, at the same time enhancing the sense of complementarity and completeness. The Holy Spirit seeks only the opportunity to minister to whatever needs are present in a marriage, and in their moments of prayer together a couple give Him entrance into opened hearts and minds. God fulfills His design for Christian marriage when lines of communication are first opened to Him." [2]

HUMILITY IS NEEDED IN PRAYER

"How can one approach God in marriage more realistically through real prayer and real communication? Couples frequently are totally unrealistic in their prayers. Often they look for something that just doesn't happen to most people. They are looking for God to take over their partner and straighten him out, cure him of his bad habits, coerce him into being what they want their partner to be. Prayer offered with this motivation does not fit into the context of the New Testament at all. It certainly does not fit into the context of humility and love as it is described in the Scriptures by God Himself.

"Humility means that one is committed to the reality that he is not always right and the idea that one is never all right in the complexity of personal differences. But most important is the fact that a humble person is a teachable person; he is capable of learning from and through his experience.

"Real prayer and communication with God begins with humility and recognition of dependence on God.

"Prayer can be meaningful if we only stop dictating to God and stop asking Him to put His stamp of approval on our own outline of the problem. We need to approach God with humility and say, 'Lord, we're in trouble. Help us. Help us to realize what we can do to make this a better marriage.'" [3] *

* From *Everything You Need to Know to Stay Married and Like It* by Wiese and Steinmetz. Copyright © 1972 by Bernard R. Wiese and is used by permission.

PRAY TOGETHER FOR HARMONY

"Communication is the means by which we learn to know and understand our mates. God, however, already understands our mates; he created them. Let us ask him to open our channels of interpersonal communication and give us the same understanding that he has, that our marriage relationship may grow increasingly precious every day." [4]

"There is a sense in which marriage is a three-story affair. There is a third floor of the spiritual where we worship together, where we appreciate God together, where we pray together. If we disagree here, a certain disunity will seep down into the second floor, which is our emotional and mental state. This will lead us to disputes, mental and intellectual debating and haggling; and this division on the second floor naturally seeps down into the physical relations of the first floor and takes the deepest desire from them. Everything that is crowned, is crowned from above! Unless in the marriage relationship there is an 'above,' some spiritual rapport, it is difficult for the physical relationship to be at its best." [5]

PRAYER

1 Samuel 12:23	As for me, far be it from me that I should sin against the Lord by ending my prayers for you; and I will continue to teach you those things which are good and right.
John 16:24	You haven't tried this before, [but begin now]. Ask, using my name, and you will receive, and your cup of joy will overflow.
Philippians 4:6	Don't worry about anything; instead, pray about everything; tell God your needs and don't forget to thank him for his answers.
1 Thessalonians 5:17	Always keep on praying.
James 5:16	Admit your faults to one another and pray for each other so that you may be healed. The earnest prayer of a righteous man has great power and wonderful results.

THE HOLY SPIRIT IN YOUR MARRIAGE

But when the Holy Spirit controls our lives he will produce this kind of fruit in us: love, joy, peace, patience, kindness, goodness, faithfulness, gentleness, and self-control.

Galatians 5:22, 23

Marriage

1. Lessor, Richard. *Love and Marriage and Trading Stamps.* Chicago, Ill.: Argus Publishers, 1971, p. 7.
2. From Dr. Wayne Oates. Source unknown.
3. From a message by Dr. Robert Shaper, Fuller Theological Seminary at Forest Home Conference Grounds.
4. Smith, Sydney. *Lady Holland's Memoir,* Vol. I. London: Longman, Brown, Green and Longman, 1855, chapter 10.
5. Augsburger, David. *Cherishable: Love and Marriage.* Scottsdale, Pa.: Herald Press, 1971, p. 16.
6. From Elton Trueblood. Source unknown.
7. From a message by Dr. David Hubbard, President of Fuller Theological Seminary.
8. Harnick, Bernard. *Risk and Chance in Marriage.* Waco, Tex.: Word Publishers, 1972, p. 17.
9. Rodenmayer, Robert N. *I John Take Thee Mary.* New York: Harper and Row, 1956, p. 18.

Love

1. Liebman, Joshua. *Peace of Mind.* New York: Simon and Schuster, 1946, p. 71.
2. Maugham, Somerset. *The Trembling of a Leaf.* New York: George H. Doran Company, 1921, chapter 4.
3. Cole, William. *Sex in Christianity and Psychoanalysis.* New York: Oxford University Press, 1955, p. 231.
4. Fromm, Erich. *The Art of Loving.* New York: Harper & Row, Publishers, 1956, p. 56.
5. Ibid., p. 128.
6. Overstreet, Harry. *The Mature Mind.* New York: W. W. Norton & Company, Inc., 1949, p. 103.
7. Ford, Edward. *Why Marriage?* Niles, Illinois: Argus Publishers, 1974, p. 103.
8. From a message by the Reverend Bob Lee at Talbot Theological Seminary Chapel.
9. Clinebell, Howard. *The Intimate Marriage.* Nashville, Tenn.: Abingdon Press, 1970, p. 219.
10. Katz, Robert. *Empathy—Its Nature and Uses.* Glencoe: The Free Press, 1967, p. 1.
11. Ibid., p. 5.
12. Ibid., pp. 7, 8.
13. Simons, Joseph and Jeanne Reidy. *The Risk of Loving.* New York: Herder & Herder, Inc., 1968, p. 108.

Communication

1. Howe, Reuel. *The Miracle of Dialogue.* New York: Seabury Press, 1963, p. 3. Adapted.
2. Small, Dwight H. *After You've Said I Do.* Westwood, N.J.: Fleming H. Revell Company, 1968, p. 75.
3. Howe, Reuel. *Herein Is Love.* Valley Forge, Pa.: Judson Press, 1961, p. 100.

4. Small, p. 75.

5. Ibid., p. 81.

6. Howe. *Herein Is Love,* p. 99.

7. Lobsenz, Norman M. and Clark W. Blackburn. *How to Stay Married.* New York: Cowles Book Company, Inc., 1968, p. 66.

8. Augsburger. *Cherishable,* p. 55.

9. Ibid., pp. 67, 68.

10. Howe, Reuel. *The Creative Years.* New York: The Seabury Press, 1958, p. 69.

11. Mace, David and Vera Mace. *We Can Have Better Marriages If We Really Want Them.* Nashville: Abingdon Press, 1974, pp. 98–99.

12. Howe. *Herein Is Love,* p. 99.

Listening

1. Tournier, Paul. *To Understand Each Other.* Richmond, Va.: John Knox Press, 1967, p. 29.

2. Dr. Samuel Hayakawa.

3. Howe. *Creative Years,* p. 74.

4. Small, p. 119.

5. Earnshaw, George L. *Serving Each Other in Love.* Valley Forge: The Judson Press, 1967, p. 80.

6. Wright, H. Norman. *Communication: Key to Your Marriage.* Glendale, Calif.: Gospel Light Publications, 1974, p. 55.

7. Augsburger, David. *Man, Am I Uptight!* Chicago: Moody Press, 1970, p. 118.

8. Ibid., p. 120.

9. Rogers, Carl R. and Richard E. Farson. "Active Listening" (unpublished paper).

10. Ibid.

11. Koehler, George E. and Nikki Koehler. *My Family: How Shall I Live With It?* Chicago: Rand McNally & Company, 1968, p. 57.

12. Ibid., p. 62.

13. Ibid., p. 69.

Truth

1. Lederer, William J. and Dr. Don D. Jackson. *The Mirages of Marriage.* New York: W. W. Norton & Company, Inc., 1968, p. 108.

2. Small, pp. 59, 60.

3. Whiston, Lionel. *Are You Fun to Live With?* Waco, Tex.: Word Publishers, 1968, p. 121.

4. Ibid., p. 123.

5. Augsburger, David. *Caring Enough to Confront.* Glendale, Calif.: Regal Books, 1974, p. 89.

6. Strauss, Richard L. *Marriage Is for Love.* Wheaton: Tyndale House Publishers, 1973, p. 85.

7. Mace, p. 103.

8. Fairchild, Roy W. *Christians in Families.* Richmond: The CLC Press, 1964, p. 147.

9. Augsburger. *Man,* p. 14.

10. Ibid., p. 15.

11. Augsburger. *Caring,* p. 13.

Understanding

1. Tournier, p. 29.

2. Fairchild, p. 149.

3. Tournier, p. 30.

4. Ibid., p. 59.

5. Shedd, Charlie W. *Letters to Philip: On How to Treat a Woman*. Garden City, N.Y.: Doubleday & Company, Inc., 1968, pp. 82, 83.

6. Harnick, p. 17.

7. Lobsenz, p. 66.

8. Bower, Robert K. *Solving Problems in Marriage*. Grand Rapids: William B. Eerdmans Publishing Company, 1972, p. 41.

Sex

1. Tournier, Paul. *Secrets*. Atlanta, Ga.: John Knox Press, 1965, p. 47.

2. Shedd, Charlie W. *Letters to Karen*. Nashville, Tenn.: Abingdon Press, 1965, p. 111.

3. Augsburger. *Cherishable*, p. 97.

4. Earnshaw, p. 66.

Forgiveness

1. Whiston, p. 116.

2. Fairchild, pp. 172, 173.

3. Small, pp. 149, 150.

4. Becker, Wilhard. *Love in Action*. Grand Rapids: Zondervan Publishing House, 1969, p. 29.

5. Earnshaw, p. 84.

6. Augsburger. *Cherishable*, pp. 141, 142.

7. Augsburger, David W. *Seventy Times Seven*. Chicago: Moody Press, 1970, p. 40.

8. Becker, p. 30.

9. Ibid., p. 29.

10. Evans, Louis H. *Your Marriage—Duel or Duet?* Old Tappan, N.J.: Fleming H. Revell Company, 1972, pp. 98, 99.

Criticism

1. Augsburger, David. *Be All You Can Be*. Carol Stream, Ill.: Creation House Publishers, 1970, pp. 74, 75.

2. Hubbard, David. *Is the Family Here to Stay?* Waco, Tex.: Word Publishers, 1971, p. 32.

3. Anonymous.

4. Anonymous.

5. Anonymous.

6. Lessor, p. 67.

7. Benjamin Disraeli.

8. Thomas Jefferson.

9. Augsburger. *Seventy*, p. 97.

10. Ibid., pp. 97, 98.

11. Ibid., p. 99.

12. Ibid., p. 100.

Anger

1. Menninger, William C. "Behind Many Flaws of Society, Families That Fail to Function." *National Observer*, August 31, 1964, p. 18.

2. Augsburger. *Be All*, pp. 31, 32.

3. Wright. *Communication*, p. 90.

4. Augsburger. *Caring*, p. 49.

5. Ibid., p. 48.

6. Wright, H. Norman. *The Christian Use of Emotional Power*. Old Tappan, N.J.: Fleming H. Revell Company, 1974, pp. 112, 113. Adapted.

7. Ibid., pp. 113, 114. Adapted.

8. Ibid., p. 127.

Disagreements

1. Small, p. 137.

2. Ibid., p. 154.

3. Mace, p. 89.

4. Wiese, Bernard R. and Urban G. Steinmetz. *Everything You Need to Know to Stay Married and Like It*. Grand Rapids: Zondervan Publishing House, 1972, p. 45.

5. Small, p. 137.

6. Ibid., p. 139.

7. Fairchild, pp. 169, 170.

Prayer

1. Tournier, Paul. *The Healing of Persons*. New York: Harper & Row Publishers, 1965, pp. 88, 89.

2. Small, p. 244.

3. Wiese and Steinmetz, pp. 36, 37.

4. Strauss, p. 87.

5. Evans, p. 76.

61464